Kip Went Zip

by Sydnie Meltzer Kleinhenz
illustrated by Jackie Snider

Scott Foresman

Editorial Offices: Glenview, Illinois • New York, New York
Sales Offices: Reading, Massachusetts • Duluth, Georgia
Glenview, Illinois • Carrollton, Texas • Menlo Park, California

Kip saw Kim go.

Kim did not see Kip go.
Kip went zip.

Kip ran to pick up a ball.

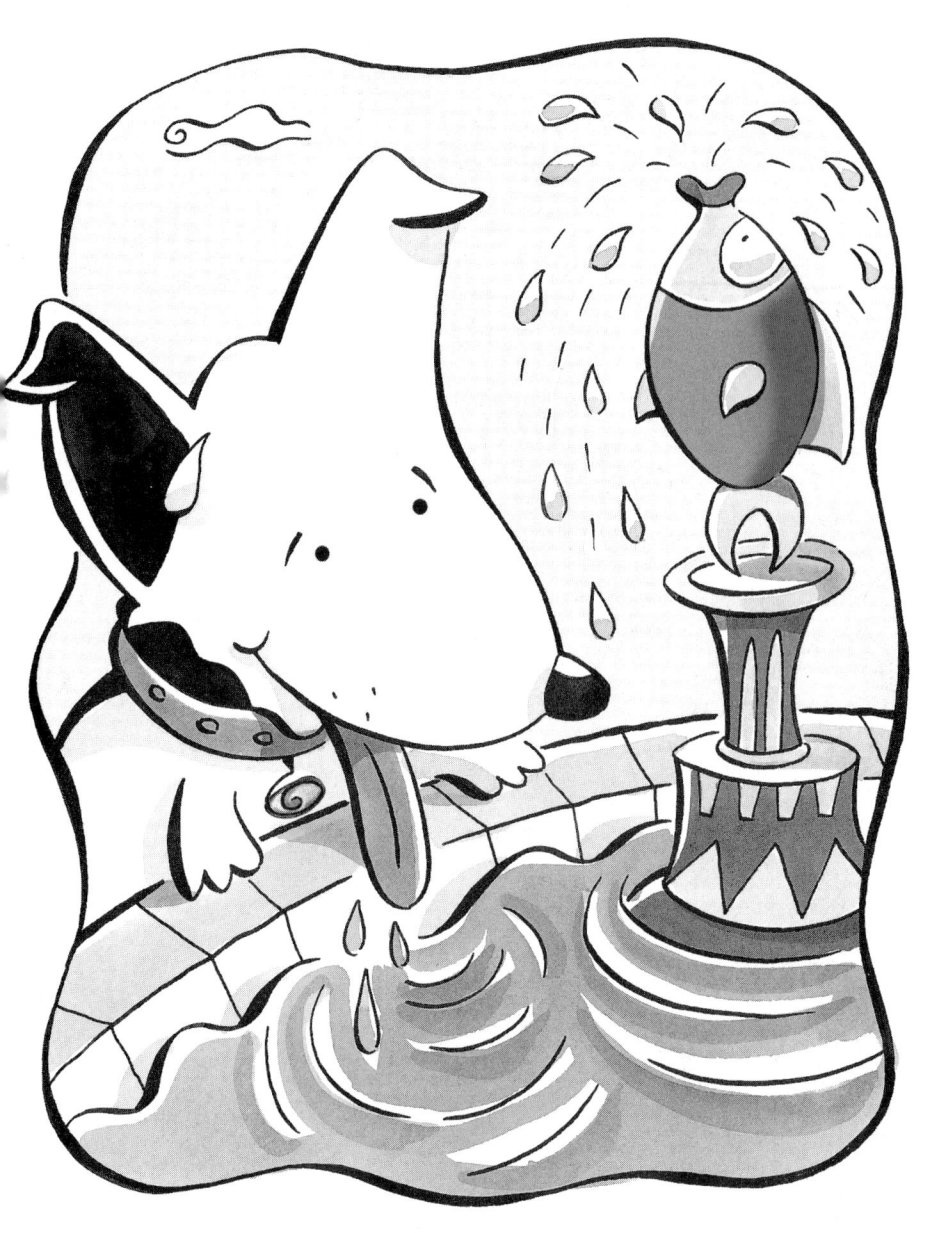

Kip ran to get a sip.

Kip ran to lick a rib.
Kip bit it.

Kip saw Kim.

Kip ran back.

Kip went zip.

Kim did not see Kip go zip.
Will Kip have a walk?
Will Kip go zip?